1 MONTH OF
FREE
READING

at
www.ForgottenBooks.com

By purchasing this book you are eligible for one month membership to ForgottenBooks.com, giving you unlimited access to our entire collection of over 1,000,000 titles via our web site and mobile apps.

To claim your free month visit:

www.forgottenbooks.com/free1341046

ISBN 978-0-365-09905-5
PIBN 11341046

Contents

Environmental Protection goals that were met in fiscal 1988 included continuing to get wastewater treatment plants upgraded for full compliance with federal laws. The Game and Fish Division was allotted a new $15 million lands acquisition budget to improve wildlife-related recreation in Georgia, including hunting and fishing. Opposite page, Georgia Parks added major improvements and new facilities statewide, including golf courses and convention lodges; and programs of the Coastal Resources Division continued to enhance and protect the State's marshes and beaches, and the valuable recreation and commercial opportunities in this region.

Introduction

As our State moves toward the 1990s, for many it is a time of remarkable prosperity. A favorable economy, mild climate and strategic commercial location have contributed to fortuitous growth in recent years. Georgia's natural and environmental resources remain a cornerstone of the State's prosperity and high quality of life.

Since its organization as a branch of State government in 1972, the Georgia Department of Natural Resources has, in accordance with State and federal laws, been responsible for managing and promoting the wise use of Georgia's air, land and water resources, its abundant fish and wildlife, the unspoiled 100-mile coast and marshlands, and all State parks and historic sites. State and federal grant programs are administered by the Department to provide public services, as well as natural resource development, management and protection in individual communities. The Department's four major operating Divisions are Environmental Protection, Game and Fish, Parks, Recreation and Historic Sites, and Coastal Resources.

The Board of Natural Resources is the Department's governing body, and is comprised of 15 members, each appointed by the Governor for staggered, seven-year terms and confirmed by the State Senate. A board-appointed Commissioner, approved by the Governor, is chief executive for the Department and serves as Director of the Environmental Protection Division.

State funds appropriated by the General Assembly, some federal grants, and monies generated by the Department to fund approximately 25 percent of operating costs, comprise the Department's yearly budget. A total of 1,515 positions were budgeted as of calendar year 1988.

In 1987, as part of the Department's ongoing Five Year Strategy for Managing Natural Resources, each major Division completed a comprehensive five-year management plan presenting specific goals for the coming five years, to be revised yearly. The goals set by each Division will help achieve a workable balance between the conservation and supply of natural and environmental resources. This report presents detailed progress on Departmental objectives, goals and priorities concerning these resources today.

Goals Under DNR's Five-Year Strategy
For Managing Natural Resources

Environmental Protection Division

• A plan for regional public water supply reservoirs throughout North and Central Georgia to ensure adequate water for essential uses in times of drought;

• Implementation of a Groundwater Management Strategy to maintain and improve Georgia's groundwater quality and availability;

• Development and implementation of a Statewide Toxics Management Strategy, to decrease risks of the public's exposure to toxic pollutants.

• Other important goals pursued in 1988 were attaining compliance with federal standards for the air pollutant, ozone in metropolitan Atlanta; getting all hazardous waste treatment, storage and disposal facilities in Georgia under enforceable permits as quickly as possible; and moving cities with inadequate sewage treatment facilities into compliance with federal standards by July 1, 1988.

Game and Fish Division

• Acquisition of suitable lands for wildlife management and public fishing areas;

• Identification of future law enforcement needs and development of required skills to meet these needs.

Division of Parks, Recreation and Historic Sites

• The upgrading of all State parks and historic sites to a high standard of quality;

• Acquisition of lands and development of new park facilities to meet the increasing demand for recreation opportunities in the State.

Coastal Resources Division

• Enhancement of coastal marshes and sand-sharing systems;

• Improvement of recreational angling opportunities in the region;

• Upgrading of existing programs for Georgia's commercially important crustacean, finfish and shellfish.

DNR Special Programs

The Georgia Nongame Wildlife Conservation Program and the Georgia Natural Heritage Inventory are dedicated to identifying, protecting, improving and restoring habitat for Georgia's nongame, rare and endangered plants and animals.

Environmental Protection

Through financial assistance, technical advisement, and environmental planning leadership, the Environmental Protection Division (EPD) helped Georgia communities meet the many challenges that accompany intensive growth in fiscal 1988, by implementing a wide variety of programs to protect and effectively manage environmental resources.

Georgia's environmental programs operate within the framework of 21 State and federal laws to protect and improve air, land and water resources that are in increasingly higher demand in our State, which is the fifth fastest-growing in the nation. Programs administered by EPD enlist the involvement of local governments and citizens, encouraging them to take an active role in environmental planning and problem solving. The awareness that natural and environmental resources are finite, and in everyone's care, has emerged as an important realization for Georgians, especially in the past decade, during which regions of our State have experienced some of the most pronounced commercialization and residential growth that has taken place in the entire nation.

During the year, controls on potentially harmful air emissions were strengthened again to help further curtail pollutants from growing numbers of automobiles and new industries in Georgia. To maintain water quality, EPD continued assisting with the upgrade of all wastewater plants in the State, while promoting wastewater disposal alternatives

and sounder treatment plant operations. Larger populations, combined with prolonged droughts, have stressed our State's traditionally plentiful water supplies, and assuring adequate water while protecting its quality were major challenges facing EPD and local communities. Solid and hazardous waste disposal issues were addressed during the year, and EPD continued examining waste-to-energy projects and other options that will result in waste reduction and recycling.

Disbursements. The Division distributed $8 million in environmental assistance grants under the Georgia Environmental Grants Program during the year, helping some 150 communities build or improve environmental facilities. Of these monies, $1 million funded emergency water and sewer improvements; $2 million funded solid waste management projects; and $5 million supported economic development opportunities. Twenty-four of the 55 communities that received economic development grants were also assisted with loans from the Georgia Environmental Facilities Authority.

The Division administered federal grants totaling $36,503,020 for wastewater treatment system improvements. In a massive effort, Georgia's communities have spent $1.4 billion to improve wastewater and sewer systems since 1973. Because federal funds for these projects will soon be depleted, a State Revolving Loan Fund (SRF) has been set up for self-perpetuating, low-interest loans.

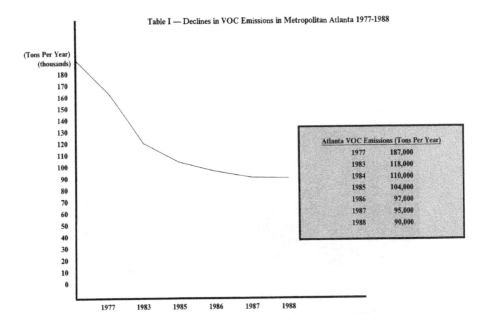

Table I — Declines in VOC Emissions in Metropolitan Atlanta 1977-1988

(Tons Per Year)
(thousands)

Atlanta VOC Emissions (Tons Per Year)	
1977	187,000
1983	118,000
1984	110,000
1985	104,000
1986	97,000
1987	95,000
1988	90,000

Air Protection

Except for the ozone problem in metropolitan Atlanta*, Georgia again met all State and federal air quality standards in fiscal 1988. Atlanta's continuing ozone problem is Georgia's only persistent air quality issue. In attempts to solve it, EPD has required increasingly stricter emission controls. In the past decade, more than 83,000 tons per year of volatile organic compound (VOC) emissions from industries and vehicles have been eliminated in the metropolitan Atlanta area. Since 1979, approximately $750 million has been spent to lower VOC emissions in the Atlanta area, mostly by industries.

In 1988, EPD further tightened the regulations for controlling VOC emissions. VOC emissions measured in the metro Atlanta area have steadily declined as a result of increasing restrictions, as shown in Table I.

During the year, EPD also gathered new data on more than 400 existing industries that potentially contribute harmful emissions to Georgia's air. If it is determined that any industry needs further controls to eliminate the possibility of toxic effects, EPD will revise that industry's air quality permits accordingly.

Because of increasing restrictions on air emissions, over 83,000 tons of pollutants have been removed from Atlanta's air yearly over the past decade.

(*Ozone, at ground level, is a potentially harmful gas that forms when certain air pollutants from vehicles and industries combine in the presence of sunlight. The Atlanta area is one of about 70 other metropolitan areas in the U.S. with ozone levels that fail to meet National Air Quality Standards set by the federal government.)

Waste reduction and recycling can help offset the need to site additional sanitary landfills, such as this one. Inset, aluminum cans for recycling.

Land Protection

Solid waste management practices have been significantly improved since the early 1970s, through strict regulations and a State grants program. Since 1974, more than 600 solid waste management grants totaling $21.5 million have been awarded to cities and counties to help improve their programs. Today, many areas face growing waste production, diminishing landfill capacity, and difficulty in siting new landfills. Community efforts to reduce or recycle waste are minimal, and new federal regulations are expected to significantly boost waste disposal costs. These problems must be solved cooperatively by State and local governments, area planning commissions and the public.

In fiscal 1988 EPD began a program for encouraging the recycling of waste oil in Georgia. EPD also permitted the State's first medical waste incinerator and granted $100,000 to local governments for studies of potential energy conservation projects, such as "waste-to-energy" plants that burn garbage to generate steam or electricity. However, even with effective source reduction and recycling, well-managed sanitary landfills will still be necessary. Twenty-seven landfills were issued operating permits in fiscal 1988.

The passage of an amended Georgia Solid Waste Management Act during the 1988 session of the General Assembly authorized EPD to effectively regulate large volumes of out-of-state waste, which may arrive in Georgia if a national trend of shipping wastes out of the Northeastern U.S. to other states continues. Other new legislation also regulates construction on closed landfills, and the siting of new waste disposal facilities.

Georgia remains the only State fully authorized by the U.S. EPA to operate its own hazardous waste management program. As of fiscal 1988, 73 percent of the 89 industries now in Georgia that treat, store or dispose of hazardous wastes had been issued permits. Georgia has been a leader among states in getting all hazardous waste facilities under strict operating permits. All permitting will be complete in 1989, well ahead of federal deadlines.

EPD also conducted detailed investigations of 61 inactive waste disposal sites, which may contain some hazardous wastes. Based on study findings, EPD has recommended that the U.S. EPA consider eight sites for possible Federal Superfund clean-up. EPD oversaw the removal of more than 5,750 tons of hazardous wastes or contaminated soils from seven other clean-up sites.

Georgia's surface mining industry expanded

One of the Department's major goals in 1988 was to get local water supply reservoirs under development. This one, under construction, will serve the community of McDonough, in Henry County.

significantly in fiscal 1988. Surface mining is regulated under the State Surface Mining Act, which provides for environmental protection and for reclamation of all disturbed lands. Since 1969, more than 49,401 acres have been permitted for surface mining in Georgia. Reclamation activities have been completed on 14,778 acres. During fiscal 1988, 506 surface mining permits were active, 44 of which were issued during the year.

Water Management And Protection

Water Supply. Georgia has traditionally had a plentiful water supply. However, in no other area have the pains of growth been felt as sharply as in the management of the State's water supplies. These "growing pains" have manifested as water shortages during droughts, overpumping and even depletion of some groundwater supplies. The need for public awareness concerning water conservation has been urgent. Although the water shortages may appear to have developed swiftly, State government has anticipated them for several years. During fiscal 1988, EPD saw the first fruits of efforts begun in 1983 to help regions severely affected by drought secure adequate water, as communities began developing water supply reservoirs and a plan was chosen to assure adequate water for the fast-growing metro Atlanta area.

By completing siting studies throughout Georgia for 108 potential water supply reservoirs, EPD paved the way for 30 counties to secure water through the year 2020. Matching State grant funds for reservoir design were awarded to four communities during the year. The communities which were actively developing reservoirs by the end of fiscal 1988 are shown in Table II.

For years, EPD has informed citizens, industries and governments in the Atlanta area that conservation and water supply planning are crucial for this

Table II — Local Water Supply Reservoir Developments Underway in 1988

City or County	Status of Development
Homer/Banks	Land Purchased
Newnan/Coweta	Under Construction
Clayton County	Under Construction
McDonough	Under Construction
Henry/Spalding	Land Purchased
Cherokee	Being Designed
Covington/Newton	Land Purchased
Carrollton	Under Constructionn
Monroe (City)	Being Designed
Fayette	Land Purchased
Douglasville/Douglas	Being Designed
Cleveland/White	Under Construction

region, which relies mostly on water from the Chattahoochee River and Lake Sidney Lanier. During the year the Division briefed the Congressional Delegation on alternatives for meeting Atlanta's water supply needs. The Delegation is now developing legislation for Congress to authorize using Lake Lanier to provide more water for the metropolitan area. This will give Atlanta a reliable drinking water supply through the year 2010.

Legislation enacted in 1988 included agriculture in EPD's water withdrawal permitting program for the first time. Permit applications were sent to 2,000 Georgia farmers. EPD expects to issue about 10,000 agricultural withdrawal permits. Permitting will protect farmers, allowing them to secure the water they need for crop irrigation.

EPD substantially increased the monitoring of public drinking water for volatile organic chemicals and other contaminants during the year. Reports show that no community's supplies are contaminated by organic chemicals. The Division also

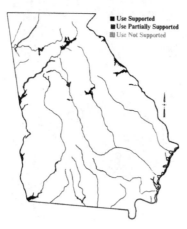

■ Use Supported
■ Use Partially Supported
▥ Use Not Supported

Figure 1. Waters Not Fully Supporting Designated Uses as of 1988
(From the Georgia Clean Water Report, 1988)

conducted a lead monitoring survey during the year which showed that Georgia's drinking water supplies have, if any, very low levels of lead.

Water Quality. Through its strong water quality programs, EPD continued the clean-up of all Georgia's rivers, streams and lakes. This critical task has been addressed on an ongoing basis since 1973 and has cleaned up almost all streams, rivers and estuarine waters. Figure 1 reveals the three percent of waters left that do not fully comply with federal water quality objectives. Most recent improvements have resulted from municipal wastewater treatment plant upgrades, assisted with federal funding. Though federal funds will no longer be available for such projects after 1994, the Department of Natural Resources, in cooperation with the Georgia Environmental Facilities Authority, has established a State Revolving Loan Fund (SRF) that provides low-interest loans. Of the State's almost $40 million federal grants allotment, $28 million was used to start up the SRF. EPD anticipates that 10 projects will be funded with these loans. The State contributed $5.6 million as the required 20 percent match to earn these funds for local governments. In addition, the Georgia Environmental Facilities Authority program, which has assisted over 120 communities with low interest loans, received another $20 million from the General Assembly.

Congress reauthorized the Federal Clean Water Act in 1987 to emphasize managing toxic pollutants, nonpoint source pollution, stormwater discharges, and state funding of continued sewage treatment

The quality of Georgia's streams and rivers has improved dramatically since 1973, primarily because of extensive wastewater treatment plant upgrades. Currently, all but about three percent of the State's waters meet national water quality goals.

upgrades. In response to these changes, EPD developed and implemented a Clean Water Strategy, presented in 1988, which contains long-term goals to maintain high quality water.

In April the Division also completed an assessment of water quality. The resulting report, *"Georgia's Clean Water 1986-87,"* shows the condition of all the State's lakes, streams and rivers. More than 97 percent fully support all the uses they are designated for. Figure 2 shows the relative percentages of pollution sources which caused impairment of waters in 1988. EPD has located these sources and actions are in progress to correct them. The Division aggressively pursued corrective actions in fiscal 1988, with the objective of cleaning up, by the end of 1989, all streams not fully supporting their designated uses.

EPD also emphasized correcting problems from nonpoint sources of pollution in fiscal 1988. These pollution sources are often hard to identify, and include urban runoff from streets and parking lots, chemical-laden runoff from farmlands, and excessive erosion and sedimentation from activities such as construction. The Division developed a solid management plan to address these pollution problems during the year.

Fiscal 1988 also saw a review of the State's water quality standards. Significant changes to Georgia's standards were made to strengthen control of toxic pollutants. Toward this end, the number of such pollutants regulated in Georgia was increased from eight to 65.

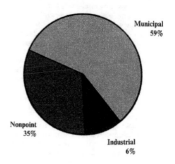

Municipal
59%

Nonpoint
35%

Industrial
6%

Figure 2. Water Pollution Sources In Georgia

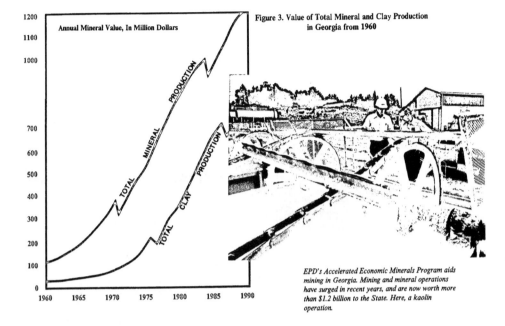

Figure 3. Value of Total Mineral and Clay Production in Georgia from 1960

EPD's Accelerated Economic Minerals Program aids mining in Georgia. Mining and mineral operations have surged in recent years, and are now worth more than $1.2 billion to the State. Here, a kaolin operation.

Geologic Survey

EPD's Geologic Survey Branch investigates Georgia's geologic, mineral and water resources. In fiscal 1988, the Survey published 18 reports or articles describing its technical investigations. Continuing drought conditions in Georgia's piedmont and mountain regions prompted the Survey to help communities locate additional groundwater supplies. Thirteen communities were assisted, and well sites recommended averaged additional well yields of 100 gallons of water per minute.

During 1987 the value of mineral products in Georgia increased to almost $1.2 billion. The economic value of mineral production in Georgia is shown in Figure 3. To aid this industry's growth, the Survey completed the third year of its Accelerated Economic Minerals Program, which included investigations for titanium, platinum, gold, clays, and construction aggregate.

Program Coordination

In 1986, Congress passed the Superfund Amendment and Reauthorization Act (SARA) to identify hazardous chemicals, which, if released uncontrolled into the environment, could pose substantial danger to public health and safety. This law makes local governments responsible for preparing emergency response plans to handle hazardous chemical accidents. With Assistance from EPD and the Georgia Emergency Management Agency, more than 85 percent of Georgia's counties developed adequate local chemical emergency response plans in fiscal 1988.

EPD maintains a highly-trained Emergency Response Team to handle environmental emergencies and assist local officials. During fiscal 1988, the team received 1,158 spill notifications, 158 of which required field investigations.

Summary

Georgia's programs to keep air, land and water resources clean and in adequate supply benefit every community and every citizen. By cooperatively working with EPD to meet environmental challenges, local governments and individuals are helping meet the demands of growth and maintain the high quality of life enjoyed throughout Georgia.

9

Game and Fish

Georgia's first MARSH water-fowl impoundment project (inset) is on the Rum Creek Wildlife Management Area in Monroe County. Several more are planned throughout the State. The areas provide habitat for resident and migrating waterfowl such as Canada geese (large photo).

Georgia's abundant wildlife, freshwater fish and native plants are among the most valuable and irreplaceable of all our natural resources. In recent years, widespread land-use changes have cost many species their habitat. These losses have prompted many Georgians to become aware of the fragile "life web" in our State's open areas, woodlands and wetlands. As a result, game and nongame management goals have been focused to conserve wildlife for its aesthetic and economic value. The Game and Fish Division enforces laws that protect and promote the wise use of all Georgia's native fish and animals and certain native plants, and conducts ongoing, comprehensive programs to improve the recreation value these resources offer.

Acquiring more lands for wildlife related recreation is a top priority under the Department's Five Year Strategy, and suitable lands have been pursued diligently. During fiscal 1988 the Georgia General Assembly approved a general bond issue that resulted in the allotment of $15 million for the purpose of acquiring additional lands for wildlife management. This new land acquisition budget, increased 30-fold over the previous budget, is now one of the highest among wildlife agencies in all 14 Southeastern states, and places Georgia in a position to be a national leader in acquiring needed lands for wildlife habitat.

Continued progress was made during the year toward acquiring more suitable lands for wildlife management and public fishing, and identifying new law enforcement needs while developing adequate skills to meet them. These goals were framed in 1987 as part of DNR's Five Year Strategy for Managing Natural Resources. They are intended to offset the loss of thousands of acres of wildlife habitat yearly, provide additional lands for wildlife-related recreation, and help ensure that the growing number of Georgia outdoorsmen recognize, and comply with, regulations for the benefit of wildlife and people.

Revenues from the last recorded year's sale of Georgia hunting and fishing licenses exceeded $13.7 million. Surveys show that anglers spend $400 million yearly, and that hunters contribute about $185 million each year to our State's economy. Wildlife oriented recreation and related equipment sales are also important sources of income for countless Georgia merchants and landowners.

Land Acquisition

Efforts to add to public recreation lands through the land acquisition program were significantly strengthened during the year with the previously mentioned approved sale of general obligation bonds, and the General Assembly agreed to consider another bond issue of the same size in 1989. The 20-year bonds will be repaid with funds generated from a 1987 increase of hunting and fishing license fees. Current land prices and interest rates make near-term acquisitions of large tracts of land desirable. Lands considered attractive are those with major river frontage; wetlands; lands with endangered plants and wildlife or areas that are ecologically unique; and areas potentially suitable for waterfowl.

The first bond sale occurred June 1, 1988. At current prices, this should allow the State to acquire approximately 42,000 acres of land for public hunting, fishing and other wildlife-oriented recreation. Land suitable for construction of public fishing lakes is also actively being sought.

A consultant to locate property and handle related land acquisition business was retained during the fiscal year. Properties that meet established acquisition criteria are actively being sought.

Horse Creek Wildlife Management Area in Telfair County is the site of many managed hunts each year. Popular game on the area include deer and wild turkey (inset).

Game Management

During fiscal 1988, over half a million hunters went afield in Georgia, and it is documented that 60 percent of Georgians enjoy wildlife through activities such as birding, outdoor photography, and hiking and camping.

Game Management operates 65 wildlife management areas (WMAs) that include over one million acres. Approximately 45,450 hunters used these areas during the 1987-88 season. The WMA program is popular among hunters as well as fishermen and other users who spend time on these lands. DNR pays lease fees to private landowners who allow their properties to be used for wildlife management.

Game Management's professional foresters oversee timber management at State-owned wildlife management areas, public fishing areas and parks. Aside from bringing revenues, timber management creates diversity of wildlife habitat and helps maintain a healthy forest community.

Canada goose and wild turkey stocking programs continued during the year. DNR stocked 900 Canada geese, primarily in Georgia's piedmont and coastal plain regions. Since 1978, nearly 13,000 Canada geese have been stocked and at least 20,000 geese are now resident in Georgia. The Department will stop releasing geese, manage existing flocks and allow limited hunting of selected populations in 1989. Under DNR's successful turkey stocking program, 196 birds were stocked on 15 sites in fiscal 1988. Turkeys now occur in all but a few metropolitan counties. Hunting was allowed in 115 counties during 1988, and Georgia's turkey population now numbers about 250,000.

During fiscal 1988 Game Management participated in DNR'S Nongame Wildlife Conservation Program, coordinated through the Commissioner's

Talbot County's Big Lazer Creek public fishing lake (inset) was completed in 1988, and will be open to the public this summer. Many more such lakes are planned throughout Georgia.

Office. Game Management also conducted surveys on wood storks, alligators and heron.

Game Management enhances wetlands for waterfowl species through the Matching Aid to Restore States' Habitat (MARSH) program of Ducks Unlimited. The first MARSH project impoundment for waterfowl on the Rum Creek Wildlife Management Area, near Forsyth, was completed in 1987. Three additional impoundments have been approved at two WMAs, and construction was begun during 1988.

Game Management continued to assist landowners with animal nuisance abatement. Information was distributed on wildlife management plans for game and nongame species, and educational programs concerning Georgia's native wildlife, such as Project Wild, helped train primary and secondary level school teachers to present basic wildlife management principles to students. The section also continues to survey all major wildlife species to identify and resolve specific problems encountered in managing Georgia's wildlife.

Fisheries Management

The Fisheries Section manages freshwater fish populations in more than 4,000 miles of trout streams, 12,000 miles of warmwater streams and one-half million acres of impoundments. Freshwater sport fishing is the most popular recreation activity in

Georgia, and some 1.5 million people participate in the sport yearly. Freshwater fisheries are a valuable source of income for Georgia. They are enhanced through private and public waters management; public fishing areas; trout production and stocking programs; warmwater hatchery production; research and surveys; and boat ramp construction.

Forecasts show that by 1990, the demand for fishing trips to small lakes in Georgia will exceed available supply. To help offset the shortage, Fisheries Management continued efforts to acquire more land for public fishing lakes. Identification of potential fishing lake sites was completed during 1988 and the Division plans to acquire the best of these sites using general-obligation bond funds. The new lake located on Big Lazer Creek WMA in Talbot County was completed during 1988 and will be open for public use in summer, 1989.

Fisheries assisted Georgia pond owners by conducting over 2,000 field investigations during the year and providing approximately 6.7 million fish for 2,900 ponds. DNR remains the only agency providing fish to private pond owners in the State. Under public waters management, the Fisheries Section uses standardized sampling to identify problems and research needs, with less expense and manpower required by intensive studies. All major reservoirs are sampled and stream and river sampling programs were developed to ensure high-quality habitat for fish.

About 100,000 trout fishermen take more than 3.8

million trout fishing trips yearly in Georgia. Trout habitat is limited to approximately 4,000 miles of streams, and native trout populations cannot support such heavy use. To help meet the demand for trout fishing, State hatcheries grow to catchable size and stock about 650,000 trout annually.

Seven warmwater hatcheries also produce fish for public waters. Major species include striped bass and striped bass/white bass hybrids. Over 400,000 striped bass and 3.3 million hybrids were produced and stocked by State hatcheries in fiscal 1988.

Fisheries research and survey programs continued to assess the condition of all fisheries, identify management needs and evaluate program effectiveness during the fiscal year. Projects included surveys of fish populations in 19 reservoirs or streams, trout stocking and hatchery production studies and others. To improve fishing waters access, the State continued to build and maintain public boat ramps.

Law Enforcement

Conservation rangers enforce laws concerning native game and nongame animals and fish, non-native animals, protected plants, boating safety, and mandatory hunter safety. Officers also support other State enforcement agencies on request. While routine duties have increased for conservation rangers in recent years, their enforcement records have continued to improve. Within the past decade, rangers have generated 126 percent more cases and warnings of violations; a 100 percent increase in convictions; and a 237 percent increase in fines. Local court systems and citizens have contributed greatly to these improvements, as have expanded education and training for officers.

The Turn in Poachers Program (TIP) rewards people who report certain Game and Fish Code violations leading to the arrest and conviction of offenders. The program received 15 percent more calls in fiscal 1988 than in the previous year. Albany State College completed a pilot research project on deer poaching in the Albany Law Enforcement District during the year, which led to establishment of criteria for a Statewide enforcement research

project in 1989. The project will evaluate information received from persons involved in a variety of major game and fish violations, and use the results to improve training and enforcement tactics.

The section also worked with DNR's Environmental Protection Division during the fiscal year to implement and enforce new laws concerning marine toilets in vessels on Lake Lanier. The 1988 General Assembly passed legislation restricting the dumping of sewage from such marine toilets into the lake.

Governor Harris' Drug Suppression Task Force continued to receive support from conservation officers in fiscal 1988, and 45 volunteers received civil disturbance management training. The DNR team assisted police at the Democratic National Convention.

Summary

DNR's Game and Fish Division has made great progress in efforts to acquire lands for wildlife management, and upgrade law enforcement in Georgia to improve wildlife resources and related recreation. These objectives are being met during a period of widespread land-use changes, many of which disturb valuable wildlife habitat. Because of management actions taken during the year, Georgia's abundant wildlife resource, as well as wildlife habitat and related recreation, will be improved and will continue making a valuable contribution to the quality of life in Georgia.

F.D. Roosevelt State Park, cabin on lake. Left, wild azaleas.

Parks, Recreation And Historic Sites

Growth in numbers of visitors to State parks and historic sites has been as pronounced as the growth seen in any other segment of Georgia's economy in recent years. During fiscal 1988, Georgia State parks and historic sites hosted a record 13,717,135 visitors and brought the economy nearly $10 million in revenues — an indication of health for Georgia's tourism industry, and one that holds the promise of new opportunities for underdeveloped areas in Georgia.

Georgia's parks and historic sites, covering 61,000 acres of natural beauty, are expected to continue to draw visitors at a growth rate three times that of the national average for state parks. Our State's increasing attraction for residents and vacationers should continue well into the 1990s. To enhance their economic potential and to improve the recreation experience Georgia offers, extensive upgrades of the entire parks system were begun in 1987 as part of DNR's Five Year Strategy for Managing Natural Resources. In addition to the goal of upgrading all parks to the highest possible standards, the acquisition of new lands and construction of new facilities is a priority that will enable the State to meet the increasing demand for public recreation in Georgia.

The Department is pledged to develop a quality State parks system not only for economic benefits, but also to assist in the goal of preserving Georgia's diminishing natural areas for present and future generations.

Grant Disbursements. The Division's Funding Unit administered Federal Land and Water Conservation grants in fiscal 1988 totaling $325,000, awarded to 13 local governments for improving or building public recreation facilities. The State's Recreation Assistance Fund awarded $555,000 to 55 municipal, nonprofit, commission, or county organizations for public recreation projects.

The Historic Preservation Section disbursed State grants totaling $349,723 and administered the disbursement of $94,100 in federal grants in fiscal 1988, to support the preservation of historic buildings and districts in Georgia.

Operations

The Division's 58 parks and historic sites, and five region offices, are supported by the Operations Section for budgeting, personnel, training, visitor services, concessions management, interpretive programs and exhibits.

Operations is expanding, with three additional lodges slated to open in fiscal 1989 at Little Ocmulgee State Park in McCrae, George T. Bagby near Ft. Gaines, and Amicalola Falls in Dawsonville. Approximately 8,000 interpretive programs and special events were developed by Operations during the year. Activities such as the traditional favorite Old Timers' Days, Civilian Conservation Corps reunions, and Pioneer Skills Days gave thousands of

children and adults a chance to sample Georgia mountain life, relax with old friends or learn fascinating new crafts. Music festivals, rendezvous and historical re-enactments, outdoor wildlife and wildflower programs, canoeing and backpacking trips, and Indian heritage activities brought visitors to parks and sites in record numbers. For the growing number of seniors visiting State parks, DNR has added exciting new educational programs, among them the Elderhostel Program, which hosts seniors from across the nation. An emphasis on high quality special events continues, and program participants have steadily increased as a result.

Maintenance and Construction

The increased visitation that major improvements to State parks will bring is expected to be an incentive for private sector development in many underutilized areas of Georgia. The Division's Maintenance and Construction Section has been instrumental in bringing these improvements about, as widespread projects to upgrade parks were initiated during the year.

Major new facilities and maintenance projects have been placed on a five-year schedule for completion, and files and inventories were compiled for maintenance projects at each park and historic site. The new maintenance files will enable the Division to upgrade the State park system on schedule.

Major improvements underway during fiscal 1988 included a $7.9 million, 60-room lodge and restaurant at Amicalola Falls; a $2.3 million, 30-room lodge and restaurant, swimming pool and tennis courts at Little Ocmulgee in McCrae; a $3.2 million, 30-room lodge, restaurant and 30-slip marina on Lake Walter F. George near Ft. Gaines;

the reconstruction of an 18th century blockhouse at Ft. King George in Darien, funded in part by $50,000 in private donations; and cottage renovations totaling over $400,000 at FDR, Stephen C. Foster, Unicoi, Vogel and Black Rock State Parks.

Projects in the design or planning phase during the year included a proposed resort in the North Georgia mountains; a $3 million, 33-room lodge and restaurant expansion of Red Top Mountain near Cartersville; improvements to Florence Marina in the town of Omaha to include a visitor's center, fishing pier and rest station; an 18-hole golf course at Georgia Veterans Memorial Park in Cordele; a nine-hole golf course at Gordonia-Alatamaha State Park in Reidsville; a new visitor's center at Jarrell Plantation in Juliette; and a group shelter at Ft. McAllister in Richmond Hill.

Historic Preservation

Many times, the only viable link the public has with Georgia's remarkable heritage is found in the structures built by previous generations. When such structures are preserved a community becomes larger, by incorporating what has gone before into its present-day progress. As evidenced in recent years, Georgians as never before are celebrating historic preservation's benefits, which are economic, as well as aesthetic.

A joint Georgia House and Senate Study

State Park Revenues and Attendance
(Fiscal 1988)

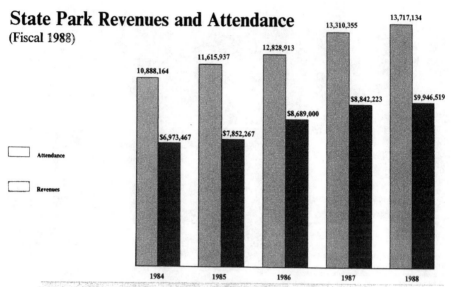

Attendance

Revenues

	1984	1985	1986	1987	1988
Attendance	10,888,164	11,615,937	12,828,913	13,310,355	13,717,134
Revenues	$6,973,467	$7,852,267	$8,689,000	$8,842,223	$9,946,519

Improvements Underway
At Georgia State Parks

Amicalola Falls $7,873,500 for 60-room lodge and meeting center with restaurant and conference room to seat 300; executive suites; road improvements. Completion spring 1989.

Little Ocmulgee $2,300,000 for 30-room lodge and meeting center with restaurant and conference room to seat 200; executive suite; pool; tennis courts. Completion, July 1988. $150,000 for an 18-hole golf course and related amenities, with architect selection in 1988.

George T. Bagby $3,200,000 for 30-room lodge/meeting center with restaurant and conference room to seat 200; executive suite; 24-slip marina; pool. Completion spring 1989.

Red Top Mountain $3,000,000 for 33-room lodge/meeting center with restaurant and conference room to seat 224; executive suite; pool. Construction start-up in September 1988.

Georgia Veterans $1,250,000 for first phase of an 18-hole golf course and related facilities. Bid in November 1988.

Mountain Resort $700,000 for design of a new mountain resort park in Towns County. Architect selected August 1988.

Jarrell Plantation $200,000 for a visitor's center. Construction begun August 1988.

Florence Marina $470,390 for a visitor's center, fishing dock; rest station. Bid in September 1988.

Ft. McAllister $240,000 for a group shelter. Construction begun September 1988.

Gordonia-Altamaha Budget, $650,000 for a nine-hole golf course. Construction begun November 1988.

Committee on Economic Development through Historic Preservation revealed in fiscal 1988 that the private sector invests $15 for every $1 of public funds spent on historic preservation projects in Georgia. Between 1981 and 1987, over $288 million in private monies have helped fund 741 rehabilitation projects, generating over 17,000 jobs. It was found that historic preservation helps communities define and enhance their image and capitalize on it for downtown and neighborhood revitalization. Economic benefits extend to industrial and business recruitment and tourism industry development.

The Historic Preservation Section conducts a variety of information and technical services to federal, State and local governments. The section helps local preservation and historical organizations, educational institutions and private citizens as well, in efforts to protect and preserve Georgia's unique cultural, historic and archaeological resources. The Statewide survey of historic structures included surveys in Thomaston and Heard counties, and nine more were started in fiscal year 1989. Forty-one Georgia nominations were added to the National Register, including 15 historic districts and 26 individual properties. Four local governments were designated Certified Local Governments, bringing to 17 the total number of governments with this qualification.

Historic Preservation gave technical assistance to the Division, including preliminary archaeological surveys at Panola Mountain, John Tanner, Sweetwater Creek, Unicoi, Amicalola Falls, Indian Springs, Ft. McAllister and Crooked River. Intensive archaeological assessments and subsurface testing were provided at Jarrell Plantation, Florence Marina and for the proposed mountain resort.

Technical Services

Technical Services issued standardized procedures for massive renovations of the park system's 3,200 campsites during the fiscal year. The section helped define and reinforce public use areas for camping, parking, picnicking and other campground activities, to help protect natural areas.

The section also developed a concept plan for the proposed resort development in Georgia's mountains. The new park's emphasis would be to bring increased economic development to North Georgia and provide the foundation for a thriving tourism industry there. The Funding Unit administered federal and State recreation grants totaling more than $885,000 (see Grant Disbursements).

The Marketing Unit completed a comprehensive, two-year marketing and promotion plan that includes a public awareness campaign for State parks. The theme, *"Georgia Parks and Historic Sites — On My Mind,"* helped creatively promote parks and historic sites in a new general brochure and individual park brochures. The unit also promoted the Georgia Parks toll-free telephone information line, and provides group market advertising and staff training to develop marketing skills for personnel.

Summary

High quality parks and historic sites will play a fundamental role in the continuing success of Georiga's tourism industry, and park developments have given substantial economic incentive to private developers. State parks and private developments can bring jobs and other opportunities to Georgians that need them.

The offering of exceptional facilities and hospitality to Georgia visitors is a goal the Department is achieving. As park improvements are completed, new and upgraded facilities will promote economic prosperity for all regions of Georgia.

Major improvements to parks in the fiscal year included a new lodge at Amicalola Falls (left). Georgia's majestic blue ridge mountains are the site for a proposed new resort, which would stimulate the economy in the already popular region.

Coastal Resources

eorgia's 100-mile coast is one of the most
ecologically unique natural areas to be
found anywhere, and its barrier islands
and beaches are among the last in our nation that
remain unspoiled. Vast saltmarshes here are the
spawning grounds for many varieties of marine life,
some species of which are endangered, or recreation-
ally or commercially important. All of these benefit
from programs for protection and enhancement.

Commercial and recreational fish and shellfish
industries in Georgia are lucrative, bringing nearly
$300 million yearly to the State's economy and
providing more than 3,000 jobs. Tourism along
Georgia's attractive, relatively undeveloped coast is
excellent business, bringing $1 billion yearly to the
State, and employing approximately 25,000 people.
Because of the coast's value to the State's economy
and the fragility of its complex ecosystem, Georgia's
shorelines and marshes must continually be
safeguarded and, whenever possible, improved.

The Coastal Resources Division, headquartered in
Brunswick, continued its many programs to enhance
marshes, beaches and sandsharing systems, upgrade
programs for commercial fish and shellfish, and
improve opportunities for recreational angling on
Georgia's coast during the fiscal year. These
programs were carried out pursuant to goals set in

1987, as part of DNR's Five Year Strategy for
Managing Natural Resources. Because Georgia's
beaches and marshlands are increasingly attractive to
visitors, developers and residents, its protection has
never before presented such a challenge. Conse-
quently, the State's permitting programs for marsh
and beach alterations are among the strongest in the
nation.

Marsh and Beach Section

Continued erosion of developed beaches in Glynn
County has generated concern from the public,
shoreline property owners, and the coastal tourism
industry. Public access to Georgia's sand beaches is
also a major concern. To help solve the problem,
DNR's Commissioner's Office, assisted by the
Governor, awarded $30,000 to the Glynn County
Commissioners to assist in a study of beach erosion
on Jekyll, St. Simons and Sea Island beaches. The
study, performed by a coastal engineering firm for
$40,000, was completed in October 1988 and
included recommendations for a beach renourish-
ment strategy for the three islands.

Georgia's "Golden Isles" beaches — Jekyll, St.
Simons and Sea Island — measure about 15 miles,

but in the past 24 years, 10.5 miles of revetments have been built on the three islands.

Shoreline recession on East Beach, St. Simons, has progressed at the rate of 30 ft. per year for the past four years. Coastal Resources Division staff has measured more than 125 ft. of landward movement of the beach escarpment since 1984. Continued erosion could threaten beach condominiums originally constructed more than 400 ft. from the ocean. More importantly, public beach access is threatened because in many areas, beaches no longer exist at high tide.

The Coastal Marshlands Protection Committee (CMPC) and Shore Assistance Committee (SAC) were each created as part of legislative acts of the same name. DNR's Coastal Resources Division serves as staff to these committees. The committees approve coastal developments and grant, suspend, revoke, or deny permits for marsh and beach construction projects. The committees each issued 17 permits during fiscal 1988. The CMPC issued five marina permits and three community dock permits. Four "mega" marinas are pending for approval in fiscal 1989. The SAC issued nine permits for Tybee Island building activities and four each for St. Simons and Sea Island developments.

Coastal Fisheries

During the fiscal year, the Coastal Fisheries Section moved toward meeting five-year goals to enhance recreational angling opportunities on the coast and improve management programs for Georgia's commercial fisheries. The four programs carried out by Fisheries include Recreational Fisheries, Outer Continental Shelf, Shellfish, and Commercial Fisheries.

The Recreational Fisheries program completed construction of inshore artificial reefs at Twin Sisters Creek in St. Simons Sound, Glynn County, and at Joe's Cut in Wassaw Sound, Chatham County. Construction began on a second artificial reef in Chatham County at Half Moon River. The reefs are constructed with an experimental design developed by Recreational Fisheries program staff, and will be evaluated as a management technique to improve sportfishing. The Recreational Fisheries Program also completed a color brochure — "Georgia's Non-Boating Saltwater Fishing Guide." The Guide will benefit residents and tourists with detailed information on fishing opportunities at public piers and bridge catwalks. A guide to coastal marinas and boat ramps in Georgia was produced jointly with the Coastal Area Planning and Development Commission. A recreational angling access plan for the coast was also completed in fiscal 1988, identifying sites for public boat ramp construction.

Research and surveys carried out by Recreational Fisheries supplied data needed to reauthorize legislation on size limits for spotted sea trout and red drum, popular sportfish species. The regulations will help ensure outstanding saltwater fishing for future anglers. A record number of people fished in Georgia's saltwaters during 1987, catching record numbers of spotted sea trout, red drum, and other fish.

The Outer Continental Shelf Program continued enhancing Georgia's offshore fishing opportunities during the fiscal year. A 55-ft. landing craft was placed at Artificial Reef "F" in September 1987. A bargeload of concrete wharf rubble from Kings Bay

Georgia's unspoiled beaches and vast marshlands benefit from strong programs for their protection. Opposite page, coastal anglers enjoy excellent recreational fishing opportunities, which the Department has worked to enhance through an artificial reef program. Inset, Angelwing seashell.

Georgia's beaches are home to many species of marine life that are sensitive to man's activities, among them the threatened loggerhead sea turtle. Sea turtles benefit from trawling efficiency devices supplied by Coastal Resources, which keep the creatures from becoming entangled.

Naval Submarine Base was placed at Artificial Reef "C" three months later. Assistance was provided to the Golden Isles Sports Fishing Club in placement of over 40 fiberglass boat molds at Artificial Reef "F."

A documentary film on CRD's Artificial Reef Program was begun during the fiscal year, and will be completed by DNR's Film and Video Unit in fiscal 1989. The film will include underwater sequences of fish utilizing reefs, as well as scenes of inshore and offshore fishermen using them. The Outer Continental Shelf Program continued working on a survey of natural reef habitat off the Georgia coast, to be used in production of a fishing guide for offshore anglers. Selection of nearshore reef sites continued, with coordination of sites with the commercial shrimp fleet to avoid trawling grounds.

Advances made in the Shellfish Program during the fiscal year have furthered the shellfish industry's development and provided for additional areas for public harvest. Water quality surveys completed for Chatham, Bryan and Liberty Counties resulted in an additional 49,000 acres being classified as public harvest areas for shellfish. Legislative changes were implemented to provide for more flexibility in setting harvest seasons for oysters and clams. With increased efforts by the Department and industries, clam landings increased 98 percent over 1986, and oyster landings surpassed 1986 landings by 127 percent.

For the second year in a row, DNR gained national recognition for operating a Shellfish Program in complete conformity with the National Shellfish Sanitation Program.

A fast growing trawl fishery for whelks, the State mollusk, produced a record harvest in fiscal 1988, exceeding one million lbs. of whelk meats. In response to the growth of this harvest, the Shellfish and Commercial Fisheries Programs initiated a research program to monitor and assess the whelk fishery.

Commercial Fisheries Program efforts in fiscal 1988 concentrated on assessing and evaluating Atlantic sturgeon stocks in the Altamaha River, and more effective management of Georgia's penaeid shrimp and blue crab fisheries. Results of a three-year research project on Atlantic sturgeon were summarized for development of legislation to give DNR capability to respond to the needs of this fishery in a more timely manner. The continued decline in blue crab landings led to the development of a research plan to investigate factors determining stock size in this important fishery. This project has received federal funding for fiscal 1989 and is expected to result in development of management strategies to ensure optimum harvest of blue crabs in Georgia.

A grant from the Georgia Office of Energy Resources enabled CRD to buy and distribute more than 800 trawling efficiency devices (TEDs) to 249 Georgia shrimpers in fiscal 1988. These devices, also known as turtle excluder devices, prevent capture and drowning of endangered or threatened sea turtles.

In cooperation with DNR's Game and Fish Division, public hearings were conducted on revision of rules and regulations governing harvest of shad in the Ogeechee River. Commercial harvest was restricted to two days per week and a recreational creel limit of two fish per angler was imposed, to reduce fishing pressure and begin restoration of the famed Ogeechee River shad fishery.

Summary

The Coastal Resources Division pursued goals framed in 1987 to safeguard and enhance Georgia's coast and vast marshlands, as prolific growth and development drew ever more attention to this fragile, unspoiled region. As programs to upgrade coastal fisheries and protect and improve beaches and marshlands continue, Georgia's coast will become increasingly popular.

While CRD programs will strengthen the valuable commercial and recreational fishing opportunities Georgia's coast offers, they will also ensure the protection of this valuable region, for the benefit of the area's ecology, and for future generations to enjoy.

The wood stork (left) and the Southern bald eagle (above) are two examples of endangered species that benefit from the protection of DNR's Nongame Wildlife Conservation program. A pitcherplant bog (right) is typical of plant communities also being protected because of threats to natural habitats.

Special DNR Programs

Georgia's Nongame Wildlife Conservation Program

The Department's new Nongame Wildlife Conservation Program, "Give Wildlife a Chance!" had a very successful first year. Private citizens, public agencies and DNR staff focused a team effort on programs to benefit Georgia's endangered or threatened wildlife.

After Governor Harris sponsored legislation that authorized DNR to establish the program in 1986, he and the General Assembly appropriated $300,000 to initially fund it. Responding to this challenge, citizens and businesses pledged corporate or cash contributions of more than $440,000 before July 1, 1988. Members of the Georgia Nongame Program Executive Committee and members of the area Blue Ribbon Committees worked especially hard to fund this special effort.

In keeping with the Department's overall goal to effectively manage all Georgia's wildlife, public education and habitat restoration programs will continue for threatened or endangered wildlife. Georgians will have the opportunity to make donations by checking off a contribution on individual State income tax forms in 1990, for taxable year 1989. These donations will be critical to the program's success. Meanwhile, continued fundraising will allow important programs to continue.

Achievements during the past fiscal year exemplify the programs that donations will support. In 1988, DNR successfully released into the wild seven bald eagles, 12 golden eagles, and successfully initiated a Statewide Adopt-an-Eagle program with 12 out of 19 eagles being adopted by organizations or individuals. In cooperation with with Zoo Atlanta, Safari Club International and the Peregrine Falcon Fund, DNR also released four peregrine falcons.

The Department raised 10 osprey chicks at various hacking facilities, initiated a Statewide bluebird restoration program and undertook several important nongame research projects on endangered species. The interpretive naturalists assigned to Georgia State parks and historic sites also significantly improved and expanded organized tours, talks and presentations relating to nongame wildlife. *(continued)*

The Hairy Rattleweed (top left) is among Georgia's rarest plants. The Georgia swampforest and fresh-water wetlands (above and below left) are examples of unique natural communities catalogued by the Georgia Natural Heritage Inventory.

The Georgia Natural Heritage Inventory

Through the Georgia Natural Heritage Inventory (GNHI), DNR continued a complete assessment of all rare natural communities found in the State, gathering critical information on rare plants and animals as they occur in Georgia, for their protection and preservation. The inventory's computer database was increased by 80 percent in fiscal 1988.

When the Natural Heritage Inventory was begun in 1986 through a joint contract with The Nature Conservancy, its goal was to identify and catalogue all plants, animals and natural habitats in Georgia that are rare enough to warrant State and federal protection. There are approximately 600 rare species being catalogued in Georgia.

During 1988, the GNHI continued collecting data on the location, status, distribution and threats to rare plants and animals, while assessing their protection needs. Approximately $15,000 in federal funds received during the year helped benefit federally protected species in Georgia, or those that are candidates for federal protection.

The GNHI has mapped and catalogued over 800 occurences of rare plants, 800 occurences of rare animals and 200 unique natural communities in Georgia. The inventorying includes vascular plants and vertebrates, as well as natural communities in granite outcrops, bogs, sandhills and forestlands. Approximately 100 natural communities under federal, State or private protection have been mapped and catalogued. Databases on the natural history and range of all vertebrates found in the State have also been developed. A computer bibliography of information sources on Georgia's rare species and natural communities was expanded by 40 percent during the year. The program also completed a report for the Governor's Growth Strategies Commission on the protection needs of sensitive natural areas in Georgia.

The Nongame Wildlife Conservation Program and the Georgia Natural Heritage Inventory will continue to work hand in hand toward conserving wildlife and natural communities in Georgia, with the help of Area Nongame Committees in all regions of the State. Everyone's support of these vital programs is most appreciated.

Summary of Expenditures

Fiscal Year 1988 Expenditures	Internal Administration	Parks, Recreation & Historic Sites	Coastal Resources	Game & Fish	Environmental Protection	Total Department
Positions	93	476	34	491	421	1,515
Personal Services	$3,281,589	$13,366,923	$1,371,941	$17,936,646	$16,403,076	$52,360,175
Operating Expenses	1,423,875	8,314,416	589,963	7,182,565	5,301,128	22,811,947
Capital Outlay	439,427	5,368,630	166,210	1,541,081	40,337	7,555,685
Contract Payments	2,274,583	1,634,746			435,000	4,344,329
Grants - Federal Funded		855,745			174,337	1,030,082
Grants - State Funded		1,095,996			8,232,556	9,328,552
Nongame Wildlife Habitat	150,000					150,000
Total Expenditures	**$7,569,474**	**$30,636,456**	**$2,128,114**	**$26,660,292**	**$30,586,434**	**$97,580,770**

Fund Sources						
State Funds Appropriated	$6,666,014	$18,233,936	$1,508,940	$21,231,571	$21,910,501	$69,550,962
Governor's Emergency Fund	10,000	291,000			232,556	533,556
Federal Funds	255,531	1,408,654	424,307	4,886,980	8,101,163	15,076,635
Self Generated Funds		10,391,856		378,679	75,963	10,846,498
Other Funds	637,929	311,010	194,867	163,062	266,245	1,573,113
Total Fund Sources	**$7,569,474**	**$30,636,456**	**$2,128,114**	**$26,660,292**	**$30,586,428**	**$97,580,764**

Bond Funding

Parks New/Major Expansions		$3,155,000				
Game and Fish Land Acquisition Program				$15,000,000		

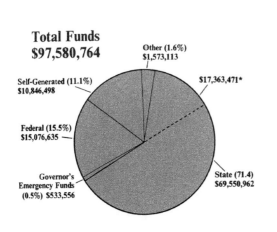

Total Funds
$97,580,764

- Other (1.6%) $1,573,113
- Self-Generated (11.1%) $10,846,498
- Federal (15.5%) $15,076,635
- Governor's Emergency Funds (0.5%) $533,556
- $17,363,471*
- State (71.4) $69,550,962

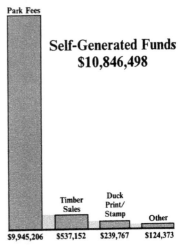

Self-Generated Funds
$10,846,498

- Park Fees $9,945,206
- Timber Sales $537,152
- Duck Print/Stamp $239,767
- Other $124,373

* Revenues derived from sales of hunting and fishing licenses and permits and recreational/commercial boating fees ($15,962,730); asbestos removal license fees ($332,864); water well drilling permits ($29,605); fines ($1,031,134); sales of confiscated items ($6,238); miscellaneous permit, etc. ($900).

For more information
on programs to enhance and
protect Georgia's natural
resources, call or write:

Georgia Department of Natural Resources
205 Butler St., S.E.
Suite 1258
Atlanta, Georgia
30334
(Tel) 404/656-3500

205 Butler Street
Suite 1252
Atlanta, Georgia 30334

404/656-3500

The Department of Natural Resources is subject to Title VI of the Civil Rights Act of 1964 and the Rehabilitation Act of 1973 and offers all persons the opportunity to participate in its public programs regardless of race, color, national origin, age, sex, or handicap. As a recipient of federal funds from the Department of Interior, the Department's programs must be operated free from discrimination. If you believe that you have been discriminated against in any program or activity or if you desire further information regarding the prohibition of discrimination, please write to: The office of Equal Opportunity, U.S. Department of the Interior, Office of the Secretary, Washington, D.C. 20240.

9 780365 099055